D1460312

WHY DOES GOD ALLOW IT?!

A. E. Wilder-Smith

Christian World Publications

12 Forrest Road, Edinburgh, EH1 2QN

Why Does God Allow It?

Copyright © 1980

Second Printing 1983

MASTER BOOKS

Division of CLP
P.O. Box 15908
San Diego, California 92115

Library of Congress Catalog
Card Number 80-80283
ISBN   0-89051-060-1

Cataloging in Publication Data

Wilder-Smith, A   E
  Why Does God Allow It?
    1. Theodicy   2. Good and evil
I. Title
                214   80-80283
  ISBN   0-89051-060-1

Printed in United States of America

*Printed by
Publishers Press
Salt Lake City, Utah*

CONTENTS

ABOUT THE AUTHOR

A. E. Wilder-Smith received his first doctorate in physical organic chemistry at the University of Reading, England in 1941. During World War II, he joined the Research Department of Imperial Chemical Industries in England, and after the war, he became affiliated with the Cancer Research staff at the University of London. Subsequently, he became Director of Research at a Swiss pharmaceutical enterprise, and was elected to teach chemotherapy and pharmacology at the Medical School of the University of Geneva. In 1964, he earned his second doctorate at the Eidgenossische Technische Hochschule in Zurich, and in 1965 he earned an additional doctorate at the University of Geneva.

In 1969, Dr. Wilder-Smith accepted an invitation to teach graduate pharmacology in Turkey. During this period, he was requested by the NATO forces to develop a series of lectures designed to combat the heavy drug abuse that was occurring within the armed forces. Since that time, he has held such lectures in universities and police academies throughout Europe and the Near East, instructing on the consequences of all types of drug abuse, including alcohol, tobacco, and psychedelic drugs.

Dr. Wilder-Smith is the author or coauthor of over 50 scientific publications, and more than 20 books which have been published in English, German, French, Russian, and Romanian. At present, he is engaged in the preparation of TV films tracing the origin of the universe and the origin of life and species.

Chapter 1

A BAFFLING STATE OF AFFAIRS

"I can't understand it," the professor said to his colleague. "It is beyond my comprehension how otherwise intelligent people can say they believe in an all-knowing, all-loving, all-powerful God and actually refer to this God as a person. These people even imagine that they have a personal relationship with this personal, loving God.

"To a certain degree," he continued, "I can understand their attitude when they see a beautiful sunrise, an orchid in full bloom, or even healthy young men and women. But they must be very naive if they do not take a look at the other side of the coin. What do they have to say about the cat that sneaks up to the mouse, plays with it, slowly tortures it, and finally devours it? Is this behavior nice, beautiful, and friendly? What about the young mother dying of cancer, her body stinking with decay before being laid in the coffin? Is that a sign and proof of God's great wisdom and love? And what about the horrors of war, especially those of today? Remember the gassing and other horrible methods used to kill God's "chosen people" — the Jews — in the concentration camps?

"Why would a kind, loving, all-powerful God not only let such abominations happen, but as the almighty one, actually ordain them? Even godless people would have put an end to

these atrocities if they had had enough
power, but this 'loving' God has let
them continue for ages.

"Tell me what you really think
about all the refined torture we see in
nature around us. Take, for example,
the process of malaria transmission. It
shows signs of what looks like careful,
well-devised planning, with the single
purpose of plaguing and torturing its
victim. To me, the whole system looks
like a remarkable plan, as if both the
good and the bad were planned for
mankind and biology. As far as I can
see, it appears that a creator, if he does
exist, is at the same time good and evil.
An almighty and good God could not
show so many evidences of what seem
to be thoughtful, planned goodnesses in
the universe and at the same time so
many signs of calculated, cold-blooded
sadism.

"Can anyone representing supreme
wisdom and goodness also be terribly
vindictive and evil, planning all sorts of
plagues and tortures for men and ani-

mals? The whole concept is complete nonsense. And so is the idea of the wicked devil competing with God and single-handedly causing these difficulties. If God was almighty and good, He would have immediately extinguished the devil, who, then, could not have clouded the issue. And if God is not able to prevent his devilry, then the devil must be equally powerful. We are then reduced to the primitive idea of warring gods in the heavens, an idea that has been erased through intellectual growth centuries ago.

"I used to say," he continued emphatically, "that I was an agnostic and therefore was not sure about these things. But now that I am older, I have come to the conclusion that, in reality, I am an atheist. I do not believe in a God, either good or bad. Such beliefs raise more difficulties than they remove, and just complicate the issue. Nowadays, I avoid these considerations in my thinking. I do not need to darken my intellect any longer with such matters.

WH • 3229

May I also add that I cannot see how any intelligent, respectable person can believe otherwise!" The professor concluded his oration with a scowl that closed the door on any further discussion.

This man's ideas reflect the questions many people are asking today. If God is God, then He must be almighty. Why then does He not bring all this chaos to a halt, all these wars, all the deception, injustice, misery, and disease in the world? If He loves us, as the Bible affirms, why does He not end all misery and produce order? If He were almighty, He could change everything immediately. He would no longer be God if He were not almighty, and if He is not that, why should we bother about Him? It is the concurrent existence of evil and good that has produced many atheists like the professor we previously quoted.

Why did God allow all of this? Does He no longer love us and care for us? Job asked the same kind of ques-

9

tions as the catastrophes befell him and his family. An all-powerful God could have prevented them — if He had wanted to. Did He, then, actually wish it to be so? Did He care about Job? If not, why should Job care about Him and continue to serve Him. Granted, there were still many things in Job's life that pointed to God's care in spite of thorns and thistles and family hardship, but there was no clear picture of God's love or care. Many signs existed *for* and *against* the existence of God's being, love, and care — just as they do today. One needs only to take a look at the world around him; the same contradictions arise now as then. Why should we believe and trust in a good God despite the evidence to the contrary? Some people say that the exercise of "faith" will eliminate this difficulty, but faith denies one of our highest faculties: the ability to weigh evidence and then to act on it. If the same Higher Being could plan both good and evil, beautiful and ugly, then all serious

United Nations/Jerry Frank

thought and human reasoning about Him becomes nonsense.

But before we continue, let us see what the Bible teaches about this state of affairs. Chapter I of the letter to the Romans clearly states that creation does not show the slightest sign of any of the above contradictions. Creation gives us only one line of thought that God is a glorious, omnipotent creator and that His universe proclaims His almighty power. "Because that which may be known of God is manifest in them; for God has showed it unto them. For the invisible things of Him from the creation of the world are *clearly seen*, being understood by the things that are made (nature), *even His eternal power and Godhead;* so that they are without excuse." (Romans 1:19-20)

Thus, the Bible teaches that if a man considers the universe and nature but does not at the same time see the power and being of the Godhead in them, then that man is "without excuse." It even goes one step further and

13

teaches that the man who sees God in
the image of His glorious creation but
does not thank and praise Him for it —
being overwhelmed with the wonders
that reveal His wisdom — that man's
thoughts will become "vain and his
imprudent heart will become darkened"
(Romans 1:21). This means that one
cannot consider nature and the universe without being overcome with
thanksgiving and worship toward the
God who reveals Himself through it.
And if one persists in refusing to see
God in His universe, one will eventu-
ally become unable to use one's higher
reasoning faculties and logical powers.
One's "heart" will become "darkened";
one will become indifferent toward reason and morality. If mankind does not
honor God upon observing His creation, then man's logical ability will
degenerate. Logic, says Paul in this
portion of Scripture, demands thanks
and worship to God. If refused, man's
logical ability will perish!

We can see that the Holy Scripture

does not show much sympathy for intellectual difficulties about believing in God. A glance at the present universe by a man of even minimal intelligence should be enough to convince him of the existence of a good and gracious God and bring about sincere gratitude and worship. How is it then that many intelligent people continue to run into intellectual difficulties which seem to make believing in God impossible? Investigation of "that which is seen" has not revealed to them "the unseen," but has, instead, often turned them from believing in anything unseen at all! For what they have seen shows so many paradoxes that, judging the unseen by what they see, God becomes impossible, ridiculous, or superfluous for further serious thought. Atheism becomes the only solution they can accept without sacrificing their intellectual integrity.

Chapter II

THE ORIGIN
OF EVIL

Do the difficulties mentioned above really arise from the facts? Does the chaotic state of nature create insurmountable intellectual difficulties which stand in the way of honest belief in God? Perhaps a personal experience can clarify these questions.

Before the Second World War, I often visited the cathedral at Cologne. I admired this beautiful piece of Gothic architecture for hours at a time — its graceful flying buttresses, magnificent high-domed roof, medieval stained glass windows, and splendid organ. The more I admired the cathedral, the more I found myself admiring the architects and masons who had, over the years, designed and built the whole structure. Obviously, the graceful lines had been carefully planned by experts possessing not only a knowledge of building mathematics but also an understanding of the principles behind beauty. The quality of their craftsmanship was first class in every way. My respect for these builders increased even more as I remembered that they possessed relatively few mechanical devices to facilitate their work. Thus, the superb structure of that cathedral showed something of the superb minds behind it. It could not have come into being without enormous planning and preparation.

During World War II, Cologne suffered perhaps the most intensive air

Cathedral at Cologne - before bombing
Rheinisches Bildarchiv

Cathedral at Cologne - after bombing
Rheinishces Bildarchiv

bombardment of any city in Western Europe. Since the cathedral stands almost directly in the railroad station yard (which was the target of frequent heavy bombing), it was often badly hit. I well remember the sadness of seeing the cathedral again in the fall of 1946. Practically every building near it had been razed to the ground, but high above the rubble the two famous towers were still standing. From a distance, the towers still seemed to be intact, but upon coming closer, one could see huge holes in the massive masonry. Hundreds on tons of concrete and bricks had been used to plug one huge hole high up in one tower, partially replacing the masonry which had been blasted away by an aerial bomb. The roof was a shambles, the organ was ruined, and everywhere lay knee-deep piles of indescribable rubble.

This miserable picture of chaos made a deep impression on me as I thought of the earlier order and beauty. While these memories were passing through my mind, I never once connected the current condition of this formerly beautiful building with any inefficiency on the part of the constructing architects or masons. Nor did I ever begin to doubt the existence of the architects merely because their handiwork lay before my eyes in shambles. Actually, the very rubble, the remnants of former beauty, showed how well the architects had planned the now-ruined structure. The mighty flying buttresses and the graceful Gothic arches were still there. Even the bombed-out holes in the walls made it obvious how well the architects had designed everything and how expertly the masons had built it. The bombs had laid bare their work, showing how well they had done their jobs. Thus, even the very ruins were witness to the good architects' and masons' work! In some ways, the ruined structure showed even better than the intact one, the perfection of the architects' plans and construction. There was no slipshod stucco or false walls such are found in many modern buildings.

Obviously, no one could accuse the architects of having produced a ruin. In general, it is quite easy to distinguish between the ruined plan and the original plan. Although the cathedral displayed both perfection and ruin, order and chaos, it would be extremely illogical to conclude that there could have been no inventive mind or architect behind it, or that one could no longer hope to recognize any characteristics of the mind or minds behind it.

This bombed cathedral brings to mind the condition of creation today. It certainly is a hopelessly mixed picture of order and chaos, beauty and ugliness, love and hate, all inextricably mixed up with one another. But, once again, it is illogical to assume that the edifice of creation has no mind or creator behind it. This is the atheist position we mentioned above. For the atheist maintains that he sees nothing but contradictions in nature. He, therefore, rejects from his world of ideas any thought of a creator behind nature. However, we dare not forget that even the tiniest island of order in the largest sea of chaos demands a creator of that small remaining order.

It is also a mistake to assume that because of the confused picture, no characteristics of a mind behind nature can be distinguished. In fact, one can often recognize design even better in a ruin than in the intact structure (as in the case of the ruined cathedral). The study of cancer cells (a good example of the "ruination" to which living entities can easily be reduced) has laid bare many secrets of the healthy intact cell, which otherwise would not have been so easily discovered.

Therefore, although creation presents a confused picture of good and evil, it is unreasonable to conclude that no Creator exists and that it cannot reflect His character. Destruction in creation often brings out the quality of the mind behind it better than its original perfect state does.

And yet atheists and agnostics maintain that a look at the world reveals nothing concerning the mind of a Creator, simply because of the hodge-podge of good and bad, the picture of order and disorder, which confuses the issue. Romans I teaches the untenable nature of just this thesis. For the Apostle Paul maintains that illness, death, hate, and ugliness are all mere outward signs of an inward state of universal "ruin." The outward signs of ruin are easily distinguished from those of health, life, love, and beauty, which still bear testimony to the original condition of things. Even the fallen creation reveals enough of the Maker behind it to bring any intellectually honest person to his knees in thankful-ness and worship. For if he sees even the smallest island of love, order, or beauty in the largest sea of hate, dis-order, and despair, he must acknowl-edge those islands with respect and worship for the One who created them.

Chapter III

WHY DOES GOD ALLOW EVIL?

Of course the illustrations which we have thus far used are incomplete. The illustration of the cathedral is no exception. Its incompleteness lies in the fact that the architects of the cathedral have long since died and could not have prevented the bombardment of their masterpiece. God is not dead, however, and the question arises as to why an almighty God who presumably loves His masterpiece (the creation), did not prevent its "bombardment."

This, then, is the question: Why does a God of love allow all the evil and not put a stop to it? This question can only be answered by defining the nature of love.

One cannot adequately discuss God's love, of course, because He and His attributes are infinite—far beyond our ability to understand. All that is infinite lies outside the capacity of our very finite thinking apparatus. So we do not propose here to explore in any depth the question of God's love or virtue. We will consider love and virtue only so far as they deal with human love and virtue, and then we will apply what we learn to the indescribable phenomenon of God's love.

Although it is impossible for human beings to realize the extent of God's infinite love, the Bible teaches that we should try to understand as much as we can about it. To help us do this, He has illustrated His infinite love through an example of finite human love. The love of the Son of God, Jesus Christ, is, for this reason, often compared to the love between a human bridegroom and his bride. Christ characterizes Himself repeatedly as the bridegroom and His children as the bride.

In an attempt to understand God's love for us through the use of this illustration, we must pay particular attention to how love between a bride and her bridegroom originates. One day, the young man meets the girl and feels an attraction to her, an attraction better experienced than described. Traditionally, the young lady does not make the first move in this relationship, but waits for the young man to do so. He begins to court her by sending her flowers or in some other suitable way. Before the courting really begins, the love affair is one-sided, and a truly one-sided relationship can be painful. The attentions must be returned if happiness and satisfaction to both parties are to result.

At this stage, there is one burning question which the young man would like answered: Is my attraction to her reciprocated? The purpose of courtship is to settle just this one question. One fine day, the young lady notices his attentions and attraction toward her and realizes that she must decide whether or not she is willing to return his affection. If she is wise, she will consider this question carefully. She may seek the advice of her parents or a trusted girl friend. Parents (and some friends) have had more experience in such matters than she. If she finally decides that she may safely return the affection, she must be sure that she can really love him totally and completely. If she can, an understanding may soon be reached between the two, and great is the joy of two hearts that have entrusted themselves to one another in mutual love, abandon, and faithfulness.

In order to better understand the process of falling in love, we must observe a few points. First, the young man must *court* the girl. If force or impatience take the place of courting, joy and love will cease. They are often replaced by hate and misery. The whole structure of love is built on mutual consent and total respect for each partner's character and freedom of will. In other words, the basis of human love is complete freedom to love — absolute free will on the part of both partners to either give or withhold their affection from one another. Without this freedom, true love is impossible.

When Eliezer, Abraham's servant, asked Rebekah to become Isaac's wife, he wanted to take her with him immediately after receiving the consent of her relatives. But the family knew it would be better if they discussed the matter with her personally. So they called a meeting of the whole clan, and only after she had expressed her own free will, did they agree to the journey and the marriage (Gen. 24:56-58). This is the basis for love and marriage in all civilized lands. Both partners of a wedding must affirm their free will decision to marry and must individually answer *"I will."*

Another important aspect of love involves the consequences of neglecting the above-mentioned mutual free will decision. The shocking love affair between Amnon and Tamar illustrates this matter (Sam. 2:13). Amnon fell madly in love with the king's beautiful daughter, Tamar, but just could not wait to woo her and win her love and consent. By deceit, he succeeded in getting her alone. In feigning sickness, he forced his "love" on her. The results of Amnon's brutal impatience was that his love turned, in a flash, to utter hatred toward her. Naturally, Tamar's heart was broken, and she "remained desolate in her brother Absalom's house." The young girl suffered much more under this animal relationship than the young man did, which shows how necessary it is for men to understand that women are individuals to be respected and held inviolate.

The point here is that if love is replaced by force, then the possibility of real love is abolished and will be replaced by hate. Absolute free will, then, is a *prerequisite* of all true love.

The Bible teaches that God Himself is love. On this basis, He looks for a free-willed responding love from us — a pure, warm, genuine love from the objects of His love. Love is only satisfied when returned free-willed love is won. God is not constrained in any way to love us, he just loves us because He *is* love. Such a divine love does not *force* us to return His love. The very attempt to do so would destroy the basis of all real love and all real virtue. As our true lover, God does everything possible to prove the genuine nature of His love, even to becoming a fellow man in the person of Jesus Christ. Of His own free will, God (in Christ) died for us to free us from guilt and sin.

God's Word says that greater love has no man than that which lays down a life for his friend (John 15:13). But Jesus Christ, as He courted man, went even further than this. He laid down His life for His *enemies*, thus demonstrating the greatest love of which man is capable.

Now consider one more vital point in our discussion of free will and love: What would have happened if God had so created man that he could not make a true free-will decision for himself, but was capable only of automatically doing God's will . . . just as a lock opens when one turns the correct key in it or as a vending machine delivers the bar of chocolate when the correct coin is inserted. If man had been so constructed that he delivered love and goodness whenever God pushed the right button, would he be capable of love or any other virtue? Could a system of real love have been produced in which man was so created that he was automatically virtuous, loving, kind, and incapable of sinning? Assume that God, in order to be sure of our love, had taken away our free will, so that we could only love and never hate. He presses the button and we automatically deliver "the goods" — our love. Could such a creation in any way involve real love? If God had made us so that we could not hate, could we ever really *love*? The necessity for absolute free will in making decisions — to love or to hate — is inherent in any creation in which love and virtue are to exist.

Because God, being love, decided to create the possibility of true love among men, He had to take the chance that His intended partners in love would not love at all. God's eternal plan is to set up a kingdom of real love on earth and in heaven. But reaching this end involves a built-in risk — that of hate and vice arising instead of love and virtue. It is usually the person who has not considered this aspect of love who wants God to turn into a dictator and use brute force to *forbid* all of the evil that exists. But this person doesn't seem to realize that if He did, He would at the same time *destroy all possibility of true love in our world.*

Exactly the same risk is involved in planning any other virtue. Take, for example, the virtue of generosity. When a poor man begs for money to buy a meal, and I give him something, I am doing something good. On the other hand, when the city authorities send me a tax bill to help the poor and needy, it becomes my *duty* to pay. In this type of "giving," I no longer exercise a virtue, even though the poor man may receive exactly the same amount of money he would have in the first instance. The difference is that in the first case, I gave of my own free will. In the second, I paid taxes because it was my obligation to do so. Therein lies no virtue; forced "charity" is not charity at all, but a duty. This is the basic error of all socialist and communist plans to produce a paradise on earth. Their schemes are destined to produce vice, not virtue. If I force my children to be good when we are out visiting, they may be outwardly polite and well-mannered, but I must recognize the fact that this "goodness" may not even be skin deep! Force itself can make no one good or virtuous. It may be very satisfactory punishment for wrong-doing, but in itself does not make anyone really good.

This thought discloses the weakness in our present socialized world: Most works of "charity" and "works of love" have been taken over by the State. Thus, real works of love and true charity are abolished as soon as the basis of free-will offering is removed. The socialist and communist state becomes a loveless, virtueless institution. The free-will donator of money and goods obtains a "blessedness" or happiness through his voluntary giving. Jesus Himself remarked that it was more blessed to give than to receive. The exercise of any virtue ennobles and enriches the character, giving real joy and radiance to the one who exercises it. The taxpayer, on the other hand, pays his taxes because he *must* do so. In the modern state, being forced to pay taxes — even for "charity" — results in little happiness or enriching of the character. This is one of the basic reasons why life in a socialist state, which allows no freedom of action but controls every facet of life, generally robs its citizens of virtue and strength of character.

Many orphan homes throughout the world used to be supported and staffed completely by free-will offerings and services. These homes full of young victims of suffering were real havens of love and joy to thousands of orphans. But nowadays, many such private institutions have been taken over by the State and are supported by taxation. The result is often that the personnel of such institutions, instead of creating an atmosphere of love, are as cold and devoid of love as the concrete blocks of the walls which surround

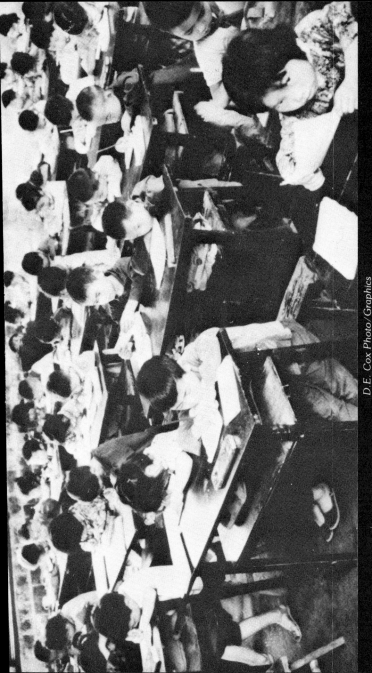

them. The welfare state, in taking over everything (in an attempt to remove some real abuses), too often kills real love and the other virtues which are dependent on freedom and which, previously, were the driving strength of the private institution. Of course, private institutions can be loveless, too, but generally speaking, by removing the freedom of service on a voluntary basis, love and joy evaporate. This disastrous effect has been already imprinted onto the character of many modern nations and is nowhere more clearly seen than in totally socialized communities.

This absence of free-will service paves the way to dictatorship, which has, as a chief requirement, lack of noble character in the mass of the citizenry. The strength of character necessary to withstand any tyrant is not likely to develop in any generation without the ennoblement of character resulting from long-term voluntary exercise of the various human virtues we have discussed. The modern socialized world tends to suppress just these character-building elements by adopting a false humanitarian attitude ("free" provision of every need "from the cradle to the grave") in dealing with many of life's problems. A consequence of these facts is that even fewer men will possess the strength of character necessary to be ready and willing to suffer for conscience's sake in resisting the totalitarian demands of the socialist state.

When God created the celestial worlds and its angels, He planned on the very best; that is, a world of true love and virtue. To do this, the very first requirement is, of course, complete freedom of choice for the inhabitants of that kingdom. Accordingly, the angels and their leader, Lucifer, were given natures capable of free choice between good and evil. Thus, they were capable of genuine love toward their Creator and toward their fellows. They were capable of coveting His love and of being wooed by Him. This capability brought, of course, the corresponding possibility that they would reject God's love. The Bible reports that a large proportion of the angels followed Lucifer when he decided not to love and turned his back on his Creator's love. By rejecting the God of love, Lucifer and his angels became loveless; that is, hateful, envious, and vessels of all the vices which are opposed to the virtues summed up in God's character of love.

Thus, the very existence of evil in a world created by an almighty and loving God demonstrates that the good and the virtues in it really are genuine. The love in it is true love and nothing else. The presence of real evil in God's world is evidence enough that God is truly a God of real love.

After Lucifer had made his decision against the God of all love, he began to seek companions for himself. Accordingly, he approached Adam and Eve, who were also capable of love and, therefore, possessed free choice. They,

too, turned their backs on the God of
love. They, too, became evil, introduc-
ing vice, sin, and suffering into man's
realm, for to turn one's back on love
and virtue is to turn one's face toward
vice, greed, and hate.

Does the above not show the high
esteem in which God holds His
creatures? He takes our free-will decisions and our love very seriously . . . seriously enough to court our
love in good faith. Love always es-
teems and respects the freedom of its
partner. This explains why God calls
men by the method known as "the
foolishness of preaching" and not by
sending, as He could, mighty angels or
superior intelligent creatures with His
message. If they appeared in their
supernal splendor, perhaps they would
only succeed in terrifying humanity,
and fail to win men's hearts by a
free-will decision. God's real purpose
is to win man's trust and love. For
this reason, He uses natural, gen-
tle methods to persuade us. He does

not browbeat us with authorative demonstrations. Such would be the method of a dictator, but not that of a lover. He employs no methods that would force mankind to accept His love, for one cannot terrorize people into love. The miracles that Jesus performed were designed with just this end in view — how often did Jesus forbid the recipient of a miracle of healing to publish the fact!

Thus, we conclude that God allowed the universe to be "bombarded" because the plan was to establish a realm of free choice. The bombardment was merely the confrontation with a choice to do good or evil. Only in this way could a realm arise which was capable of genuine love and virtue. The construction of a kingdom of love, a kingdom of perfect freedom, involved the built-in risk of a kingdom of hell. Without this true possibility of a free-will decision for heaven or hell, one can never establish the best — the perfect kingdom of love.

Chapter IV

GOD'S OPTIONS

What could God do after His creatures had taken the bad road by turning their backs on the only good? What were the options left open to Him?

The Scriptures say that even before the wrong choice had been made by either man or angels, God, being omniscient, knew all about it and had even drawn up careful plans in advance to cope with the consequences. God's knowledge of the wrong choice and its consequences long before it took place has been a stumbling block to many. Actually, however, few intellectual difficulties are involved in this matter if it is carefully thought through.

If I observe a person attentively during a period of time, I may notice some of his little idiosyncrasies. He may say "ah," for example, as a prelude to every difficult word he has to pronounce. Or he may twitch his eyebrows before relating a good joke. Gradually, on account of these observations, I learn to predict what he is going to do before he actually does it. However, my ability to foretell what he will do in no way makes me responsible for his actions. Similarly, the fact that God was able to foresee what Adam and Eve and mankind in general would do, does not necessarily make Him responsible for their actions, especially in view of the fact that He gave them the free will to act. God foresaw the fall of angels and men, and saw it so well that even before He had brought creation into being, He was prepared to send His son as the sacrifice for the wrong choice (sin). Yet many people imagine that God's foreknowledge of the fall must somehow make Him responsible for it. In fact, quite the contrary is the case. Man was given a truly free will, and with it came the possibility of real love and virtue . . . or real hate and sin. This fact decides forever the creature's genuine guilt in the face of the Creator's love and righteousness in making man in His own image, that is, capable of independent choice and, like God, capable of real love.

At this point, the question may arise that if God saw in advance the chaos and awful possibilities of misery, hate, and suffering conferred on man with the gift of free will, why did He proceed to create us? Was He not rather sadistic to have persisted in those plans if He knew in advance the shocking results? Would it not have been better to have dropped the plan of creation before starting to create, if it was going to work out as terribly as it has?

The same type of questioning arises every day in our own lives, as for example in our decision to get married. On the very day of our wedding, we know that one day the pain of separation from our partner through death is inevitable. We accept this future loss of joy because we believe that the present ennoblement of character in giving ourselves to the other in love even for just a single day is better than no love at all. In marrying, we accept the utter misery of certain separation and death as the end of marriage, because we believe that one day of love and joy is worth more than the ultimate separation and misery at the end of marriage.

Evidently, God also feels this way, because in order to have the possibility of some love, joy, and virtue, He accepted the accompanying certainty of hate and vice. It is a question of balance. Those who have known love will admit that it weighs infinitely more than the distress which its freedom may bring with it. Apparently, the Creator, the God of love, agrees — for He went ahead with our creation in spite of the foreseeable mess which would result. He was convinced that the warmth of true love is worth infinitely more than the bitterness of suffering. Where life is, the opportunity to love exists, too.

We shall escape the trials and sufferings of this life at death, but our character of love (ennobled through our trials) will continue to live forever. So whichever way we look, we must admit that the creation, if it produced the possibility of love, is quite worthwhile, even if suffering may be involved. For love is the greatest of all virtues and far surpasses the misery which the freedom to love may entail.

Now that the fall has taken place and sin and anguish are in the world, what would we expect God to do? What does a lover do who has been misunderstood and rejected by the object of his love? The Scriptures say that love "suffereth long and is kind . . . is not easily provoked, thinketh no evil . . . beareth all things . . . endureth all things . . . never faileth." (I Cor. 13:4-8). We expect true love to be longsuffering, kind, not easily provoked, enduring all things in the hope of the ultimate success of the wooing process of love.

God saw man's wrong choice which would lead to chaos and anguish long before the choice was made. When it did come, however, He did not disgustedly dismiss and destroy the object of His love, as one might expect of someone treated unjustly. Instead, through loving patience, He tried to salvage what He could out of the ruins. In faithfulness and sternness, He had warned of the consequences of the wrong choice, but He did not block the way back to Himself by attempting to force us to return. That would cut off all possibility of winning us back to love and thus defeat His main purpose in creating man: to insure a love relationship with Him. So He exercised longsuffering and patience in trying to win us freely back to love and reason. This process climaxed in the sending of His own Son to freely lay down His life for all of us. The Son went to His death so that love conditioned His death. Never once did He try to defend Himself, but, as He said, came to die freely for the sins of the world.

Even today, He is patient with us, desiring that *all* men ". . . come to the knowledge of the truth." (I Tim. 2:4). Again in 2 Peter 3:9, His longing for us is emphasized: "The Lord is not slack concerning His promise, as some men count slackness, but He is long-suffering to us, not willing that any should perish, but that all should come to repentance." This means just what it says. It does not suggest that all men *will* repent, but that God is ready and willing to receive all who turn to Him and thereby reverse the effects of Adam and Eve's turning their backs on Him

— the Source of all good. The man who chooses God is no longer subject to the sin nature he inherited from his first parents.

The fact that God has waited so long after the "bombing" of His handiwork before judging the "bombers" is yet another indication of His true character. It proves that he is indeed a God of loving kindness, patience, long-suffering, and is not easily provoked. This is the only adequate explanation for the fact that God, the almighty, omniscient, righteous One, has not long ago exercised crushing judgment on all of us and set up a "puppet state" on earth and in heaven which carries out automatically His every command. Every dictator would certainly be anxious to set up such a totalitarian state, particularly if his will had been thwarted as God's will has been. But God's will might be even more abused if He did set up this "puppet state" to carry it out by force alone. Such dictatorial measures would effectively cancel the last small measure of love possible in this fallen creation. Those men who do see the situation as it really is and who therefore turn to God to be refreshed and regenerated by His love, find that even a little of such love and refreshment is better than none at all, which would be the case if freedom of choice, and therefore of love, were taken from us.

If the Lord had judged immediately after the fall (or any other sin), many who have since repented and turned to Him would have been lost to Him and His kingdom of love forever. Thus, His patience sees its reward in every sinner who turns to God in repentance and trust for renewal of virtue and joy, counteracting the vice and death induced by Adam's wrong choice.

A story is told about King George VI and how he won Elizabeth. As a young man, the future king of England fell in love with the pretty young lady from Scotland. After a time of reflection, he approached her on the subject of a closer relationship with her, but she refused him. (It is said that the prince had never been much of a lady's man and lacked robustness in his speech, appearance and manners.)

Young George, greatly upset over this rebuff, asked his mother, Queen Mary, for her advice. She listened sympathetically to her son's tale of woe, and then told him she wanted to ask just one question before she could properly answer him. Did he really love only Elizabeth, or would he be able to consider a substitute if her refusal was final? After a moment's consideration, he replied that he wanted to marry Elizabeth and no one else. "Well then," said his mother, "there is only one way open to you. Go and ask her again." So the prince put his pride in his pocket, gathered up his remaining courage, and asked the lovely young Scottish lady again . . . only to be turned down once more.

After recovering from this second shock, he returned to his mother for counsel. Again she listened quietly, showing him every sympathy. But she asked once again, if, after this refusal, he really did still love her. George was quite clear about his feelings. He loved her and desired only her among the choice of eligible young ladies. "In that case," said his mother, "there is only one option open to you. Go and ask her again."

After some time of mental preparation, the young prince visited the pretty young Scottish lady for the third time. She had, of course, noticed how serious the prince was; his love and determination to win her had indeed been constant. And she noticed something else. His consistent love for her was beginning to kindle an answering fire in her own heart. At last, she was able to say that she loved him, too, and would like to become his wife. Thus, the story goes, began a very happy family life that lasted until the king's death.

Love begets love, but love often

has to be very patient, long-suffering, and kind until the fire is kindled in the prospective partner's heart. Once kindled, this love must be regularly tended in order to maintain the warmth of the blaze which God intends our love to be — warming and refreshing — so that both can rejoice in the happiness which love alone can bring.

But it must be remembered that there comes a time in every love affair when the final answer to the lover must be given: either "yes" or "no." One day, the courted lady may make a rejection which turns out to be final. Not only has this lady a free will to accept or to reject the wooer, but the prospective bridegroom can also decide just how long he will continue to court and when he will desist. Even this final decision to desist will, no doubt, be made on the basis of love, and will be postponed for as long as possible. But if the sought-after lady marries another, then the decision against any further courtship attempts must be made immediately.

The Scriptures say that precisely this state of affairs may be reached in the spiritual sense when God's Spirit ceases to strive with a man or woman. Certainly God is reluctant to do this, and it hurts Him to have to give up on a man forever, but it is perfectly clear that this does occur, even though it is invisible to man's mortal eye. Jesus is the lover of man's soul, but there comes a time when man can irrevocably "marry another." We can give our hearts entirely up to material matters, to social standing, to amassing a fortune or otherwise to "selling our souls," turning ourselves completely and finally away from the things of the kingdom of heaven. Then the days of courtship are forever over. The New Testament letter to the Hebrews speaks in several places of this fact (chapter 3:11, 6:46, 10:26-30). The advent of such days presents a gloomy picture and should serve as a serious warning, lest we spurn God's grace.

Chapter V
EPILOGUE

A consideration of the nature of evil and the nature of God's love leads us to believe that it is perfectly reasonable to believe in an all-powerful loving God, in spite of the terrible state of affairs in the world He has created. If God is, in fact, love, and if He has revealed Himself as a perfect man in Christ, we should actually *expect* the world to be in the position it is today. However, one can scarcely believe that God would allow His own creation to *remain* forever in its present state. He has promised to renew His whole creation and create a new earth and a new heaven where righteousness shall reign. In fact, the Bible teaches that those men and women who have tasted the bitterness and misery of making a wrong decision in turning their backs on Him, can taste the love and joy of a *right* decision. Such will play a leading role in the renewed creation. It would seem to be less likely that they will once again make the same mistake and bring suffering into the renewed world by a repeated wrong choice. It is said that a burned child shies away from fire. A redeemed sinner shies away from sin. With those redeemed sinners, God will populate His new kingdom. At present, He is courting prospective candidates for the approaching new order on earth, which will be governed by Jesus Christ. This new creation will be ruled by the One who has proven Himself to be the best qualified for such a high office: the One who loved His creation — man — enough to die for him. Most rulers demand that their subjects show their faithfulness by their readiness to die for *them*. Christ, however, died of His own free will so that those He loves might live ... forever. Certainly a kingdom founded on such principles will be well-managed and well-governed. "For He has made known to us in all wisdom and insight the mystery of His will, according to His purpose which He set forth in Christ as a plan for the fullness of time, to unite all things in Him, things in heaven and things on earth." (Eph. 1:9-10).

This plan for the fullness of time naturally refers to the reign of God's promised kingdom on earth as in heaven, under Christ Himself. Everything in this kingdom will be summed up in Christ who will wield the power of attorney there. "Then I saw a new heaven and a new earth; for the first heaven and the first earth had passed away, and the sea was no more.

And I saw the holy city, new Jerusalem, coming down out of heaven from God, prepared as a bride adorned for her husband and I heard a loud voice from the throne saying, 'Behold, the dwelling of God is with men. He will dwell with them and they shall be His people, and God Himself will be with them; He will wipe away every tear from their eyes, and death shall be no more, neither shall there be mourning nor crying nor pain any more, for the former things have passed away.' " (Rev. 21:1-4).

The participation of men in the coming kingdom has already begun here on earth for those who have allowed themselves to be saved from the present universal corruption and lovelessness, trusting in Jesus Christ who has redeemed them from their sins. Our personal, individual choice for Christ *today* decides the issue of our eternal destiny — a kingdom of perfect freedom and perfect love between our Creator and ourselves. This is God's plan since before the beginning of time, and His love begs us to accept it. What will *your* choice be?

OTHER BOOKS
YOU WILL ENJOY....

Man's Origin, Man's Destiny

A. E. Wilder-Smith,
Ph.D., D.Sc., Dr. rer. nat., F.R.I.C.

Where did we come from...and where are we going? These questions have intrigued mankind since the beginning of time. Dr. Wilder-Smith covers the entire spectrum of existence in this fascinating and comprehensive study which commences with the beginning of life and progresses all the way to man's ultimate step into eternity. A few of the topics covered are fossil evidence of man's history, dating methods of fossils, planned evolution (selective breeding), theistic evolution, and the impact of the evolution philosophy on morality and spirituality in today's society.

No. 101, Paper.

The Natural Sciences Know Nothing of Evolution

A. E. Wilder-Smith,
  Ph.D., D.Sc., Dr. rer. nat., F.R.I.C.

What is evolution? Is it scientific? Internationally renowned scientist Dr. A. E. Wilder-Smith examines the evidence and presents the conclusions in this comprehensive analysis of evolution from the viewpoint of the Natural Sciences, a field in which he possesses great expertise. Chemical origin of life, the probability of random programming of the simplest cell, and dating methods are among the topics covered in this valuable work. Recommended for teachers and college students, as well as the layman with a special interest in the study of origins.

No. 110, Paper.